Common Sense Retirement
In Uncertain Times

Tony Dale

with Jim Sullivan

Published by Tony Dale
330 East Coffee Street
Greenville, SC 29601

Copyright ©2014 by Tony Dale

Printed in the United States

Disclaimer

This publication is designed to provide accurate and authoritative information on the subject covered. Neither the author nor the publisher engages in rendering legal, tax, accounting or other professional service or advice. If expert assistance is required, the reader should seek the services of a knowledgeable, competent professional.

Guarantees in annuities and insurance products are based upon the financial strength and claims-paying ability of the issuing insurance company. Not FDIC-insured. The purchase of an annuity is an important financial decision. You should have a full discussion with your agent before making any financial decision.

Annuities are designed to meet long-term needs for retirement income. They provide guarantees against the loss of principal and credited interest, and the reassurance of a death benefit for beneficiaries.

Early withdrawals may result in loss of principal and credited interest. Any distributions of income are subject to ordinary income tax, and, if taken prior to age 59½, a 10% federal tax penalty.

Although an external index may affect your interest credited, the contract does not directly participate in any equity or fixed income investments. You are not buying shares in an index. The index value does not include the dividends paid on the equity investments underlying any equity index or the interest paid on the fixed income investments underlying any bond index. These dividends and interest are not reflected in the interest credited to your contract.

Numbers, rates and/or illustrations in this book are in no way a guarantee of what may be available to you or available in the annuity/insurance market. Product features and rates are always subject to change, and availability may vary by state.

TABLE OF CONTENTS

FOREWORD

I have known Tony Dale for more than five years now, and being around him, his energy, and his knowledge has been an unbelievably great experience. We've traveled together and worked together, and I have learned so much from being around Tony. Not only is he one of the most knowledgeable, helpful retirement income planners I've ever met, but he's one of the finest human beings I've ever known. His message is on point, and he practices everything he preaches. I only want to partner with people who are honest, have great integrity, and put others first. That's Tony to a T.

Tony grew up in Texas, where his dad was a radio pioneer, one of the real trailblazers in talk radio. Coming from that background, he has a real gift for communicating. I am blown away by his ability to take a very complicated subject, figure it out, and then present it to others in a way that makes perfect sense. That's a real gift: taking abstract ideas and putting them in human terms—terms that not only make sense but connect with our day-to-day lives. I've seen that Tony has it in spades.

He has a wealth of knowledge that he is glad to share, and he has vast experience working with seniors, retirees, and people who are thinking about their retirement. It's all about building rock-solid retirement income strategies. As we are living longer, it is more important than ever to have a plan, and prepare ourselves with income streams that supplement our Social Security. Since getting into the industry, Tony has helped thousands of people to make better decisions about retirement income planning.

What really sets Tony Dale apart from everyone else in the industry is that he understands the history of the market better than anyone I have ever met, seen, or heard. He knows all the ups and downs, the bears and bulls, the booms and busts. But more important than just knowing what happened, he also knows the *why*. Sure, there are a lot of people who can tell you about times the market went up or down, but Tony has a deep understanding of all the factors that come together to influence the stock market and the American economy.

You will get to see some of Tony's insight into the market's history of up-and-down cycles in this book. You'll also get his thoughts about many other topics that have an impact on how we plan our retirement years. Every conversation I have with Tony brings some new insight, some new idea or way of thinking about something. I know that everyone reading this will have the same experience.

Fran Tarkenton
Hall of Fame Quarterback & Entrepreneur

INTRODUCTION

Income is the Right Outcome

It has been found in studies that the greatest fear people have is running out of money in their retirement years. Another way of saying this is that people are afraid of running out of money before running out of breath. In fact, in a 2011 survey, 61% of Baby Boomers surveyed said they are more afraid of running out of money in retirement than they are of dying.

If something is that important there certainly is an argument to be made for learning how to avoid that tragic consequence. This book is an effort to lay out a new view of retirement planning; to help equip and prepare retirees and future retirees for what is facing them in these turbulent economic times. Sad to say, much of the advice being given them is frankly not good advice at all.

I don't know how you define a retirement plan, but my Common Sense Retirement definition does not include the word "risk" or "risky." My retirement dreams don't begin with the words "if" or "maybe." My definition of retirement plan uses words like "guarantee" and "safety."

My retirement plan focuses on the predictability of the income my nest egg can produce. It includes real opportunities for my monthly income to stay ahead of inflation. It also protects me and my spouse if one or both of us live a longer life than expected. It allows me to leave a legacy to my children or anyone else I choose. I don't have to surrender my nest egg in exchange for guarantees. Finally, it allows me to fully realize my retirement dreams and focus on what truly matters – time and relationships.

When properly planning for retirement, a secure source of growing *income is the outcome.*

Welcome to Common Sense Retirement planning. For many years, my radio partner Phillip Allen and I have preached a new approach to retirement planning that I want to share with you in this book. We are an alternative to the mainstream financial press that too often serves as a cheerleader to Wall Street and the conventional, misguided approach to retirement planning (which, as I'll explain is not really retirement planning!).

Who am I? A life in the prediction business...

You are driving on a long highway. The day is clear and you can see for miles down the road where everything looks open. The conditions are ideal so you decide to ramp up to 80 mph. Suddenly, a sign appears. WARNING! DANGEROUS CONDITIONS AHEAD.

You can see for miles down the road and everything appears to be normal. What the heck, why not take her up to 90?

Another sign looms before you: WARNING! DANGEROUS CONDITIONS AHEAD.

Now another sign pops up quickly: DANGER BRIDGE OUT AHEAD! STOP! Even as you slam on the brakes you know that you will be unable to avoid crashing. And as the time stands still and the crash begins, you think, *"Why didn't I pay attention to the warning signs?"*

A very similar event is looming for millions of Americans as they approach their retirement years. Although the warning signs are everywhere, in spite of the fact they have experienced what can happen to their life savings in the dot com bubble collapse in 2000 and the real estate credit collapse of 2007 and 2008, many press on the accelerator of risk without realizing that the next warning may be the final one before their financial savings are wiped out for the last time.

I have spent most of my adult life in the prediction business. As a recovering meteorologist and a current Retirement Planner, assessing risk and what lies ahead is my passion. What I see is a retirement train wreck for countless fellow baby boomers who are still being advised to take too much risk in a very uncertain world. Many will run out of money before they run out of breath. They could find themselves living in their children's basement and learning to say "welcome to Walmart" or "would you like fries with that?" Think of me as the voice in your head urging you to pay attention to the signs. Even though you can't see the washed out bridge, it's there.

Our approach is unconventional but has worked for thousands of our listeners and clients. There are five reasons why the Common Sense Retirement approach is so different from the conventional "retirement planning" approach. Here's the first.

> **Why Common Sense Retirement is so different from the conventional approach #1**
> *With Common Sense Retirement planning, you will create a reliable, increasing stream of income from your nest egg that will last your and your spouse's entire life while still having the opportunity to leave a legacy to whomever you choose.*

With my approach, I promise you will not run out of money before you run out of breath.

Wishin' and hopin' is no way to spend your retirement years

It makes me sad to talk with retirees who are afraid to spend their nest egg because of the uncertainty the future may hold. I've heard stories of grandparents deciding against going to a grandchild's birthday, graduation or other special family event because they are afraid to dip into their nest egg. Their retirement years are spent counting pennies because of their fear of running out of money before they die. They remind me of the old Dusty Springfield song from 1964 "Wishin' and Hopin'," because that is how they spend their retirement years – wishin' and hopin' their nest egg will last.

> **Why Common Sense Retirement is so different from the conventional approach #2**
> Lots of people know how to save money for retirement. Unfortunately, very few know how to spend the money they saved for retirement. This lack of knowledge and planning comes at the cost of never realizing their dreams. That is a pity. Common Sense Retirement will teach you how to spend your retirement nest egg in retirement so that you can enjoy those years without worry.

A warning: I won't always tell you what you want to hear; I will, however, always tell you what you <u>need</u> to hear!

Planning in uncertain times

The Common Sense Retirement plan prepares you for an uncertain, increasingly dangerous world. No one can predict the future. Keep in mind the eternal wisdom from the Bible:

"Do not boast about tomorrow, for you do not know what a day may bring." Proverbs 27:1 (NIV)

"The prudent see danger and take refuge, but the simple keep going and pay the penalty." Proverbs 27:12 (NIV)

Why Common Sense Retirement is so different from the conventional approach #3

With Common Sense Retirement you take refuge from an uncertain world. Your retirement is built on safety, guarantees and predictability of income. It recognizes that as you get older the "buy and hold" advice of Wall Street is no longer applicable. Your time horizon is shorter – your ability to hold on and wait for the stock market to bounce back is diminished.

Running counter to Wall Street "wisdom"

The Common Sense Retirement approach runs against the prevailing Wall Street wisdom. That has made it difficult for Phillip and I to get our message across since we are competing against millions of dollars of advertising that Wall Street spends every year.

With the Common Sense Retirement approach, be prepared for some surprises along the way – much of what you've learned before while you saved for retirement just won't work as you near and enter retirement. It is not that you received bad advice while you saved for retirement; it is just that the advice needs to change to meet the changing circumstances of your life. Put bluntly, you're getting older! Your plan horizon is shrinking. As you will learn, Wall Street fails to take that into account.

That's because with a Wall Street advisor, you don't have a retirement plan; you have an investment plan. If you've bought into the Wall Street campaign about retirement planning, your retirement dreams are at risk.

Why Common Sense Retirement is so different from the conventional approach #4

Common Sense Retirement steers you away from the Wall Street advisors who sell investment plans, not retirement plans. It will eliminate the risk that comes with a Wall Street plan.

I truly believe that by following Wall Street advice there is a good chance that you'll run out of money in retirement long before you run out of breath. Your retirement dream may become your retirement nightmare.

I don't want your retirement dream to become your retirement nightmare. That is why I wrote this book.

There *is* a better way to plan for retirement and you are holding it in your hand. Common Sense Retirement is that better way.

The Great Fleecing Machine

By reading this book you will benefit from the advice Phillip and I have been giving the listeners to our radio show and our clients for many years. You will be joining the thousands of listeners and clients who have turned away from Wall Street and found a new path to a Common Sense Retirement.

Wall Street has been called the great fleecing machine and it is the American public being sheared. Wall Street advisors and the compliant main stream financial press join the chorus telling you Wall Street sells retirement plans. It does not. Wall Street sells risk. Wall Street only makes money when you buy risk. Risk has no place in a retirement plan.

For years Wall Street has dressed up risk and minimized it using terms like diversification, portfolio theory, correlation coefficient, Monte Carlo simulations (yes, the same Monte Carlo that is the gambling center of the world!). Risk is risk. Put lipstick on it, dress it up and it is still risk. No one was more surprised than Wall Street with the most recent market crash. Their fancy financial theories and formulas didn't work when *everything* crashed. All the diversification and Monte Carlo simulations in the world didn't help the average investor.

Bottom line, Wall Street wants to sell you an *investment plan*, not a *retirement plan*. Investment plans, by definition contain risk. And risk does not belong in your retirement plan. Wall Street will never tell you this. I will and do.

A fear greater than the fear of death

Like the vast majority of us, it is likely that your number one fear concerning retirement is running out of money before you run out of breath. In fact, like many others, you may fear running out of money in retirement *even more than you fear death*. And who can blame you – *running out of money means the loss of your retirement dreams; it means the loss of your independence.* In your final years, you will find yourself scrimping and saving to make ends meet. You will have to rely on others – perhaps your children – to provide for you.

Common Sense Retirement does not put your retirement at risk.

In order for you to understand Common Sense Retirement, I must ask you to do something that is *uncommon* - forget Wall Street and all that you have heard from its advisors and cheerleaders in the mainstream financial press. I ask you to open your mind to a better way to plan for retirement.

I am not asking you to mindlessly follow my advice – far from that. My book carefully builds the case for Common Sense Retirement. It provides the *whys* of true Common Sense Retirement planning. I hope I've done this in an entertaining way that will amuse you and keep your interest. But don't let the humor get in the way of the seriousness of the message.

Finally, I won't tell you just what you want to hear. That's what other advisors do – invest in the latest, popular mutual fund and see your portfolio soar! You can have it all – hefty retirement withdrawals, a growing retirement nest egg, a pot of gold to leave as your legacy. If only it were that simple. I'll explain the tradeoffs you must make to ensure a safe, secure retirement.

The goal in retirement planning was best expressed by respected financial advisor and author William Bernstein, M.D., Ph.D., **"The name of the game is not to get rich; rather, it's to not die poor."**

Why Common Sense Retirement is so different from the conventional approach #5
With Common Sense Retirement the outcome is income. The focus moves from the potential of your nest egg to grow to the predictability of the income it can produce.

A Second Opinion Never Hurts

Let me ask you a question. Have you ever had a health issue and gotten a second opinion? I have and it saved me untold pain and expense.

A couple of years ago, at age 65, I began to suffer from increasingly debilitating pain in my left shoulder. I had a pretty good idea what was causing it. I started boxing when I was eight years old and have spent decades studying and practicing various fighting techniques. I know,

I know; it doesn't sound like a lot of fun, but, I can't help myself, I just love it. After countless hours of bag work and sparring, innumerable left jabs and left hooks, I figured my shoulder was finally wearing out.

The first doctor told me I would need to have rotator cuff surgery and I had to immediately stop punching. Wow, all I could think of was a baby boomer term from the 60s and 70s...BUMMER.

Since I have always believed in alternative medicine, I sought a second opinion from a Chiropractor. He said what I needed was to begin stretching and rehabilitating the joint and lay off the heavy bag for a few weeks. I began to see improvement but it still bothered me. Then I found a topical substance which continued the healing process.

I am happy to report that at 67 I am still doing 10 rounds of bag work with 30 second rests twice a week and have NO SHOULDER PAIN!

What would have happened if I had just gone along with the first diagnoses and treatment? Judging from several of my clients who have had rotator cuff surgery I would have been much worse off.

Here's the point: If you lost money in the last two market corrections and you're still being told to continue doing the same thing, it's time for a second opinion. I mean, didn't Einstein define insanity as doing the same thing repeatedly and expecting a different outcome?

The State of Retirement Preparation in America...or the Great Sinkhole!

With all the constant news on the economy, one would think that Americans are busy salting away their savings for retirement. We have 401k's, IRA's, 403b's, 457's, TSP's. So how are we doing?

According to studies recently quoted in CBS' MarketWatch (www.marketwatch.com), not too well:

- 36% of Americans have less than $1000 saved for retirement.
- In households making $50,000 to $75,000, only20% have saved at least $100,000
- For those making six figures, only 10% have saved at least $1 million and 40% at least $250,000.

That is a paltry amount for those who may have to make their income last for 20 to 30 years. Consider some of the risks that retirees face. Market losses, sequence of return risk, interest rates, inflation, longevity, medical and nursing home care...to name just a few!

By addressing the three most important first, you give yourself a real chance of having a successful retirement. These are:

- Market risk
- Inflationary risk
- Longevity risk

We will discuss these in detail in the third chapter.

Of these risks, inflationary risk is the most subtle.

It's like having a hole in your boat. Think about it. You are sailing along and all is well. But unbeknownst to you, there is a leak below. You eventually begin to notice that the boat is sitting lower in the water. If the hole gets larger you sink faster. Such is the almost invisible power of inflation to rob you of your wealth. History is replete with horrific examples of the scourge of inflation. Germany in the 1930s, Argentina and Venezuela now. But what about the good old USA? Well if you listen to our friends in Washington, we have low inflation. THE Bureau of Labor Statistics (the BLS) tells us it's well under 2%. Accordingly, in 2013 Social Security recipients and government retirees got the lowest cost of living increase since the 1970s.

But the real truth is at the gas station and at the checkout counter at the grocery store. Does the increasing amount of money you spend on gas and food agree with the government statistics? If you drop the L from BLS, you will be closer to the truth. They tell us that the Consumer Price Index, or CPI, has risen "only" 37% since 2000.

If that is true, please explain to me how from 2000 – 2014:

- A gallon of gas is up 176%
- Fuel oil is up 242%
- A dozen eggs is up 106%
- Ground beef is up 96%
- A movie ticket is up 95%
- Healthcare spending is up 104%

Using the bogus CPI figures means real median household income is 7.3% *below* the level of 2000. Use a more accurate measure and we are deeper into the sinkhole than the government figures would have us believe.

So what's a mother to do? On the one hand you may lose half your life savings in the market trying to stay ahead of inflation or on the other hand, only earn the puny rates banks pay on certificates of deposit (CDs). *In my opinion, there are two things a bank can guarantee. You can't lose money and you can't make money.* Here's the good news. I will show you how to use Common Sense Retirement planning to give you a chance of gains when markets rise while locking them in and suffering no losses when markets crash. That is a rock solid way to hedge against inflation.

What's ahead?

Chapter one begins with a laundry list of concerns that will shape your retirement planning. These include longevity, inflation, health care costs, nominal vs. real market returns, and the truth about Wall Street's "buy and hold" mantra. Don't get discouraged – the Common Sense Retirement approach will help you understand the roadblocks and how to overcome them.

In *chapter two* we will discuss cycles. Not tri, bi or motor cycles, but the *cycles* of life and, in particular, the cycles of the stock market. I start with cycles because if you retire at the wrong time, you substantially increase your chances of running out of money in retirement. This is called *sequence of return risk*. It can devastate your retirement nest egg. By the end of the chapter, thanks to a simple example, you will know better the damage sequence of return risk can do to your retirement.

In chapter three we will cover a little boomer history. This will give you some perspective on how the world of retirement planning changed for the worse over the last 40 years or so and how our approach makes the necessary corrections. In *chapter four* we will explain the benefits of using stock market indices (for example, the Standard and Poor's 500; the Dow Jones Industrial Averages) over the active management of stock investments by Wall Street. The fact is, most actively managed mutual funds rarely beat the simple averages. Don't worry if some of this is new to you – you'll have a good grasp of this topic once you've read the chapter. When I say my approach is "common sense" I mean it – you don't need to know math or have an extensive knowledge of the stock market to understand the Common Sense Retirement approach.

In *chapter five* we will debunk a current retirement myth – the "4% rule." The 4% rule is one rule of thumb that is downright dangerous to follow. I'll explain why. Once you combine the *sequence of return risk* I introduce in chapter two with the *4% rule of thumb* you have a retirement disaster just waiting to happen. The Common Sense Retirement approach will make sure that does not happen.

The world is a dangerous place. Unfortunately, the United States government does not have your back. The truth is the Federal government and the Federal Reserve bailed out the banks after the 2008 crash. This bail out continues to this day. Who paid for the bail out? Go look in the mirror. Taxpayers and savers have paid the cost. *Chapter six* will open your eyes.

Finally, in ***chapter seven*** I will pull all of this together for you. I will describe what your Common Sense Retirement will look like. You'll find out that it is **not** true that I hate the stock market. I do like the stock market – but only that part that goes up. I don't have much use for the down part! You'll learn that you can benefit from up (or Bull) markets and lock in your gains without having to live with the losses. Let those who have bought into the "buy and hold" approach sold by Wall Street have the down (or Bear) markets!

In the afterword, you will learn that we will have come full circle, from the risk and uncertainty of Wall Street to the safety and certainty of a Common Sense Retirement. You will also learn that a Nobel Prize winning economist sees the world much as I describe and agrees that the focus of retirement planning must be income – not asset – growth.

Now, God bless and good reading!

CHAPTER ONE

Overcoming Retirement Planning Risks

How you will benefit from reading this chapter: There are several types of risk a retirement plan must overcome. In this chapter you will learn these risks and the threat they pose to you achieving the retirement of your dreams. In later chapters we will show you how the Common Sense Retirement program helps you overcome these risks.

Retirement planning includes developing a strategy to overcome several obstacles. A retirement plan that does not address these issues correctly is no retirement plan at all! Wall Street tells you it has strategies to overcome these challenges, but it does not. The truth is that all their "strategies" involve risk and that is no way to go into retirement.

In this chapter we will consider four of the most prominent risks. These obstacles include:

- Longevity;
- Inflation;
- Long term portfolio returns – nominal versus real;
- Overcoming bear markets - the buy and hold mantra.

Longevity

It may seem strange that longevity is listed as an obstacle. Isn't a long life a good thing? Let's agree that a long, healthy life is a great thing.

Average life expectancy continues to go up. Very recently, the Society of Actuaries revised its mortality tables for the first time since 2000. Look at the change:

At age 65	Life Expectancy in 2000	New Life Expectancy
Female	85.2	88.8
Male	82.6	86.6

Keep in mind, these life expectancies are for single individuals. By definition, life expectancy means what the average single person will live to. Others will live well beyond their life expectancies. In addition, the joint life expectancies of a husband and wife are actually longer meaning it is likely that at least one of the couple (usually the woman) will live into her 90s (and possibly beyond!). That is one reason the Common Sense Retirement plan pays special attention to planning for couples and making sure the surviving partner is secure.

What does this mean? It means a retirement of 30 or 35 years will not be unusual. Unless you have chronic health problems or a terminal illness that will shorten your life expectancy, Common Sense Retirement planning does not include "die early before I run out of money" as a planning option.

For a healthy couple age 65, there is a 50% chance that one of you will live to age 92. There is a 25% chance that one of you will live to age 97! In fact, the most rapidly growing segment of the U.S. population is those age 85 and older. This will put an enormous strain on the Medicare and Social Security entitlement programs. You need to plan for a long life which includes paying a greater share of your future health care costs.

The *Wall Street response* to increased longevity is the infamous "4% rule of thumb." This rule of thumb was designed to get you to keep your retirement nest egg invested in risky stocks and bonds even after retirement.

Here is what the rule says: you can withdraw 4% of your retirement nest egg every year and adjust it for a cost of living increase and have a better than 90% chance of never running out of money before you die! In other words, keep your nest egg in exactly the vehicles that Wall Street sells – risk and all; adhere to the 4% rule plus annual inflation adjustments and you'll never run out of money no matter how long you live. Following this advice can be disastrous for your retirement. As I'll explain in Chapter 2 and Chapter 5, the cyclical nature of the stock market means the 4% rule of thumb often fails to work and can leave you with more life long after your nest egg is gone.

Bob and Martha G. arrived at my office after much of the damage was already done. Bob retired in 2000 from a company located in California. He was a rocket engineer.

The couple had a little less than $950,000 in a retirement account with a "big box" Wall Street firm. They were told to follow the 4% rule. With a 60% equity/40% bond portfolio they could safely take a 4% income, add 3% for inflation annually and have a 90% chance their income would continue for 30 years. This theory is based on the historical market average of 7%. The problem is the 7% is the nominal (in name only) return, not the inflation-adjusted return.

It also doesn't factor in what can happen if one retires into a falling market cycle – the "sequence of returns" danger.

Most of us remember only too well what happened in 2000. The "dot com" bubble burst. It was created over several years in an orgy of what Allen Greenspan, the chair of the Federal Reserve called "irrational exuberance." By 2003 the combination of stock market losses, and the income they continued to withdraw under the 4% rule, had dropped the value of their account to $400,000 and change. They were scared witless but reassured to "stay the course. The market always comes back over time." And so it did. They began to breathe a little easier and take their 4% plus 3% for inflation each year. Then the next quake shook the markets. Between 2007 and 2008 the S&P dropped 57% after adjusting for inflation.

Bob and Martha had suffered a one-two punch from the stock market.

Panic set in. Bob and Martha started drastically cutting back on both income and spending as they watched their money evaporate like dew in the desert.

By the time they came to see me, their assets had shrunk from $950K to a mere $134K. Bob was in his seventies and Martha her sixties and because he was considered "over qualified" by potential employers he was having a difficult time finding work.

I am happy to report that we have put a safety net on what was left of their life savings.

And although their income is smaller because of their losses, it is guaranteed for life for both of them and they will get raises every time we get annual gains in their account. Their only regret if a familiar one... "if only we had come to see you sooner."

The Common Sense Retirement response is to obtain guarantees that your money will last as long as you do.

Inflation

I compare inflation to a small leak in a boat. While it won't sink the boat right away, eventually the boat will sink. Inflation reduces the value of your retirement income, slowly but surely. Even at a modest 3% annual inflation rate a $1,000 annuity payment will shrink to:

Payment	In ten years at 3% annual inflation	In twenty years at 3% inflation
Value of $1,000 monthly annuity payment	$774	$554

Another way of looking at it is "how much will my monthly annuity payment have to grow to in order to buy the same amount of goods and services in ten or twenty years?" Well, here it is:

Payment	In ten years at 3% annual inflation	In twenty years at 3% inflation
What my $1,000 has to grow to just to stay even	$1,344	$1,806

The Wall Street response is Mad Magazine's Alfred E. Neuman's signature response: "What, me worry?" Wall Street will tell you that stocks are a great way to keep up with inflation! Stay invested in risky stocks and in the long run you will beat inflation. That stocks always keep up with inflation is just not true. This is especially true in the short run. Often a spike in inflation creates uncertainty in the stock market followed by a steep bear market. Losing value in your nest egg is not a particularly good way to "keep up with inflation." Just as inflation heats up, you have to climb out of a hole of market losses before you can keep up with inflation. Furthermore, the academic studies of whether the stock market can keep you ahead of inflation are mixed at best. Don't base your retirement plan on the possibility that the stock market will keep up with inflation. It is just another way that Wall Street tries to convince you that your retirement nest egg should remain in risky stocks.

The Common Sense Retirement plan protects you from the down stock markets preserving your nest egg and allowing you to take advantage of any eventual upturn in the market. Along with income guarantees you have a real chance of keeping ahead of inflation.

Long term portfolio returns – nominal versus real

Not understanding the difference between *nominal* market returns and *real* market returns is an obstacle to proper retirement planning because Wall Street uses nominal market returns to disguise what is really happening with market returns.

Nominal means "in name only" – if I tell you that the Dow Jones Industrial average went from 10,000 to 15,000 in ten years you might be impressed. That is an increase of 50%. But what if inflation averaged 5% per year during that time – suddenly that increase is not nearly as impressive. "Real return" means what you earned <u>after</u> inflation. If the real return was negative it means the real growth in the value of your nest egg was negative. That's because just keeping up with inflation the DJIA would have to finish the decade at 16,289; instead it finished at just 15,000.

Let's look at the nominal versus real returns for three of the major indices for the period 2000 through February 2014:

Index	Date high reached in 2000	Nominal 14-year Return through early 2014	Real 14-year Return through early 2014
DJIA	January 14	+31.1%	-3.7%
S&P 500	March 24	+14.0%	-16.2%
NASDAQ	March 10	-20.8%	-41.8%

As the chart above shows, as of this writing the inflation adjusted stock market high of 2000 still had not been surpassed 14 years later. That is correct – after 14 years and the bull market of the last few years, your stock market holdings are still behind when factoring in inflation. If you were a Wall Street advisor what number would you use to impress a prospective client – nominal returns or real returns? What lesson is there in this? When a Wall Street advisor is telling you the great returns you can earn with stocks, ask if he or she talking about nominal returns or real returns. The *real return* story is the one you want!

Let's look at some other extended periods of stock market history:

Period 1: On an inflation-adjusted basis, the stock market high of September 1929 would still not be surpassed by 1949! The "buy and hold strategy" obviously didn't work for someone retiring in 1929. Chances are, if you had retired during those years, you would have bailed on the market long before it recovered its previous high. What about more recent history?

Period 2: From December 1966 to December 1982 the nominal return was .8%; the real return was a **negative 65.7%!**

My point is this: you don't have a lot of control over when you retire. You may retire in the beginning of an extended bear market in which the real return devastates your retirement nest egg. That is because in addition to the withdrawals you make your remaining investments are hammered with losses. I've shown you just two examples of markets that went down and stay downed for an extended period of time – in some cases as long as a normal retirement period of 15 to 20 years. It is imperative that your retirement plan prepare you for such an eventuality. You cannot retire and just "hope for the best." You can only retire "hoping for the best but preparing for the worst." So much is beyond your control.

The Common Sense Retirement plan takes real returns into account, not nominal returns. The Common Sense Retirement plan provides real returns by protecting you from down markets and periodically locking in your gains during up markets. Wall Street's retirement plan leaves you with one alternative – "hope for the best." With the Common Sense Retirement approach you "hope for the best but prepare for the worst."

Overcoming bear markets - the buy and hold mantra

Wall Street advisors tell you to hold on through a bear market, the market will bounce back. No one knows when it will bounce back or how long it will take, but it "always does come back." Be patient, they advise you. I guess it hasn't occurred to Wall Street that as we age, we have less and less time to "be patient." Living through a long bear market at age 32, as aggravating as that is, is far different from living through a long bear market at age 52, 62 or 72! When you are 72 your sense of urgency during a bear market increases dramatically. A market cycle can last for as few as 5 and for as long as 25 years. This means you may retire into a long-term bear market and be stuck there through all of your retirement years.

Ed listens to his inner voice

Ed A. came to me in March of 2008 worried about his retirement account with a "big box" Wall Street firm. I often refer to the big Wall Street firms as the "big box" Wall Street advisors. I do this because of the impersonal nature of the services they offer their clients. The big box stores work wonderfully well when it comes to delivering good products at good prices to their customers. It doesn't work so well in the financial advisory services that should focus on their client's individual needs and goals. At 71 years old, Ed had already lost more than $150,000 in the meltdown of 2007 and 2008.

His only sources of income were Social Security, a small pension (his pension has no cost of living increases) and periodic withdrawals from his retirement nest egg. Fortunately Ed could see the danger. If he continued to take income while losing money in the market and he would run out of his savings and be forced to make do with his Social Security benefit and pension.

His nest egg was down to $490,000 thanks to his following the advice of his Wall Street advisor. A large portion of his nest egg was still in equities. He was told not to worry "the market always comes back over time, just hang in there."

Then Ed decided he needed to get a second opinion and came to see me.

In March of 2014 we met for our annual review. During the last six years Ed has withdrawn nearly
$260,000 in income. His account value today has grown to nearly $510,000...*even after taking that income.* How? We just employed a little Common Sense Retirement Planning.

Unfortunately, not everyone listens to that inner voice soon enough.

The lesson is this: as you get older the time you have to recover your *market losses* gets shorter. At age 32 as you are accumulating assets for retirement, you have time to recover from a bear market. At age 52 your time to retirement is growing shorter meaning your time to wait for a stock market recovery is also growing shorter – and the recovery time does not improve from then on!

Remember, a 50% drop in the value of your portfolio, say from $300,000 to $150,000 due to an extended bear market, means you need a tremendous bull market that increases your stock value by 100% (from $150,000 back to $300,000 involves a 100% increase!). Such gains are rare.

As your time shrinks for your retirement assets to recover from a bear market (in other words, as you get older) you need to lock in your gains and take a more sensible approach to benefitting from future stock market increases. Yes, it will involve a trade off, but all sensible retirement strategies do. In this case we will give up some upside in the stock market in exchange for eliminating the downside.

I'll describe how that is done in a later chapter.

To summarize, the proper retirement planning must address these retirement challenges:

- Longevity – the 4% rule of thumb provides false hope that your portfolio will last as long as you do. An extended bear market at the beginning of your retirement or during your retirement years can result in the devastation of your retirement nest egg.

- Inflation – the results are mixed at best that stocks are the cure for a long term bout of high inflation. In addition, a bear market and its accompanying losses will not help you keep up with inflation!

- Long term portfolio returns – Wall Street loves to give you nominal returns, not real returns. Your real return in the stock market is the only return that matters to your ability to meet the rising cost of living in retirement.

- The "buy and hold" mantra is a recipe for disaster. "Buy and hold" is advice for a long term investor. After you reach age 50, you do not have all the time in the world to wait for a Wall Street recovery. Common Sense Retirement planning takes into account the limited time we have to put aside an adequate nest egg to fund our spending in retirement.

What's ahead? In the next chapter you will see that the difference in a financially successful vs. an unsuccessful retirement may be simply one of timing and luck. That's because the stock market is cyclical. If you retire while the cycle is heading down, your chances of having a safe, secure retirement also goes down – unless you follow my advice for a Common Sense Retirement plan.

Chapter Two

On Cycles

How you will benefit from reading this chapter: *The biggest worry most retirees have is running out of money before running out of breath. By understanding and applying the knowledge in this book, you will no longer have to worry about outliving your retirement nest egg. In this chapter, you will learn about <u>sequence of return risk</u>. You will learn that if you retire at the wrong time your retirement nest egg can be devastated – you will run out of money long before you run out of breath. The only way to avoid that devastation is to understand why a proper retirement plan is built on guarantees, safety and certainty.*

In December of 1965 the Byrds' "Turn! Turn! Turn! (To Everything There is a Season)" reached number 1 on the U.S. Hot 100 Chart.

Most listeners recognized the lyrics – they came directly from the *Book of Ecclesiastes* (Chapter 3, v. 1-8, KJV). Solomon wrote the lyrics to a rock & roll hit! They read:

> *3 To everything there is a season, and a time to every purpose under the heaven:*
>
> *^{2} A time to be born, and a time to die; a time to plant, and a time to pluck up that which is planted;*
>
> *^{3} A time to kill, and a time to heal; a time to break down, and a time to build up;*
>
> *^{4} A time to weep, and a time to laugh; a time to mourn, and a time to dance;*
>
> *^{5} A time to cast away stones, and a time to gather stones together; a time to embrace, and a time to refrain from embracing;*
>
> *^{6} A time to get, and a time to lose; a time to keep, and a time to cast away;*
>
> *^{7} A time to rend, and a time to sew; a time to keep silence, and a time to speak;*
>
> *^{8} A time to love, and a time to hate; a time of war, and a time of peace.*

This famous Bible verse reminds us that everything is cyclical. There is a time for everything. There is nothing new under the sun. The writer of Ecclesiastes was merely acknowledging an age old truth.

Again, ancient wisdom from the Bible (*Book of Ecclesiastes*, Chapter 1, v. 9, KJV):

The thing that hath been, it is that which shall be; and that which is done is that which shall be done: and there is no new thing under the sun.

The stock market is not immune from cycles. It has short cycles and long cycles.

In order to understand the common sense approach to retirement planning you need to learn a few key concepts:

1. Everything is cyclical – including the stock market.

2. One of the most important retirement decisions you will make is **when** to retire.

3. If you retire at the beginning of or during a bear (down) stock market cycle, the chance of you running out of money long before running out of breath increases substantially. **Sequence of return risk** is important to understand – but chances are you won't hear it from Wall Street – it flies in the face of their "buy and hold" mantra. I'll show you an example below.

4. Wall Street does not have a solution for sequence of return risk because Wall Street makes money only when it sells you risk. Protecting yourself from sequence of return risk means you reduce risk in your retirement nest egg; you don't increase risk as you near retirement. You won't get a retirement plan from Wall Street; you will get an investment plan. A true retirement plan contains very little risk. This is especially true when you reach age 50. An investment plan offers risk and uncertainty. A retirement plan offers security and certainty.

Market Cycles

A long market cycle is also called a *secular market*. It will contain both bull (up) and bear (down) markets. A secular market can last from 5 to as many as 25 years or longer. A secular market will have ups and downs but, in the long term, it will be primarily either a bull or bear market. An example of a secular bull market is one that lasted from 1982 to 2000. During that time, the general market direction was up. However, *within* that secular bull market was the infamous 1987 crash. The Dow Jones dropped 508 points on **Black Monday**, October 19, 1987. By the time it was done, the market lost over 22% of its value in just one day. Black Monday is still discussed by those of us who lived through it. Forget buy and hold – many stock holders unable to stomach such losses sold out in the days following Black Monday.

"So what?" you ask. "My Wall Street advisor told me to just buy and hold – hang on through those temporary market drops and I'll be fine when we come out the other side. " Buy and hold is always easier said than done. Imagine being 70 years old and living through another big drop in the market – do you think you will be able to hold on? Why put yourself through that if there are the Common Sense Retirement alternatives we will discuss later in this book?

Here is why the cycles in the market are so important. If your retirement nest egg includes direct investment in stocks (either you buy individual stocks directly or through a mutual fund or via Exchange Traded Funds – ETFs), *when* you retire matters a whole lot to what happens to your nest egg.

For example, if you retired in 1982 or 1983 at the onset of a secular bull market your nest egg will be in great shape. You would have been able to make regular withdrawals from your nest egg to help pay for your retirement lifestyle. Thanks to the great secular bull market you may have found that in 2000 after 20 years in retirement, you actually have more money in your nest egg than you started with! Of course, we are assuming here that you did hang on through **Black Monday** in October 1987! Many "buy and hold" investors – especially retirees – fled the market due to the terrifying market drop. And who could blame them? As I mentioned above, imagine yourself at age 75 witnessing the catastrophic drop as your nest egg lost 22% of its value. "Buy and hold" is easy advice to give but very difficult to practice. Unfortunately, those investors who did sell out did not participate in the rebound in the stock market that followed several months later. You know the old saying, once bitten, twice shy! Buy and hold only works if you can live with the losses in anticipation of later gains. "Buy and sell out at the bottom" does not work.

Below are the stock market cycles since 1896. Note that the shortest cycle was 5 years; the longest cycle 25 years!

Cycle: Number of Years Ending in 2010 (years approximate)*	Key Events	Bull Market Cycle	Bear Market Cycle
9 years to 1906	Market peaks at 103 in 1906	148.92%	
18 years to 1924	Panic of 1907; J.P. Morgan steps in and saves economy; World War I		-4.29%
5 years to 1929	Roaring Twenties	294.66%	
25 years to 1955	Depression and World War II		1.69%
11 years to 1966	Go-Go Sixties	154.29%	
17 years to 1982	Stagflation		.83%
18 years to 2000	The Great Bull Market; Boomers come of age	1003.19%	
11 years to...?	Dot com bust (2000); Real estate and near collapse of financial system (2008)	5.82%	

*Based on Dow Jones Industrial Averages

Let's look at an example. Good Luck Bob (you'll understand why we call him Good Luck Bob in a minute) retires at the beginning of 1995 with a nest egg of $1,000,000. He plans on withdrawing $50,000 during his first year of retirement. Subsequently, he will withdraw $50,000 per year adjusted for inflation. Because he had the good luck to retire at the beginning of a bull market, by the time he dies in 2015 his nest egg has actually grown to a little over $2,000,000 despite having withdrawn a total of $1,343,500 for living expenses during his retirement years. Bob's starting portfolio actually provided him with over $3,000,000 in value between his lifetime withdrawals and what he left to his heirs. Not bad. Was Bob a genius or just lucky? Mostly it was just plain luck. We will give Bob credit for staying in stocks even when things got bumpy in years six, seven and eight, but for the most part, it was Bob's timing, not skill, which paid off.

Common Sense Retirement

But let's put Bob in an alternative universe (we'll call him Bad Luck Bob). He retires five years later into the teeth of a bear market. In his first year of retirement we discussed above, Good Luck Bob had enjoyed a 34.11% increase in the value of his nest egg. In this case, his withdrawal of $50,000 barely made a dent in his nest egg since it increased *even after* his withdrawal to meet living expenses. Not so for Bad Luck Bob. He saw his nest egg go **down** by 10.14% in year one followed by two more down years before a recovery in year four. Along with his $50,000 withdrawal, Bad Luck Bob saw his nest egg go down in three years to less than $500,000! Could anyone blame him for telling his Wall Street advisor to shut up about "buy and hold" and get him out of the market? Especially after his further losses in years two and three? Would you have the stomach to hold on? Is it any wonder that Bad Luck Bob outlives his retirement nest egg? He never had a chance! See the chart below. And, by the way, all the "buying and holding" in the world will not improve Bad Luck Bob's chances. By the end of his third year of retirement his nest egg is down to less than $470,000. In his 14th year of retirement, Bad Luck Bob runs out of money. He lives out his final years living only on Social Security.

Here is what Good Luck Bob and Bad Luck Bob earn:

Year of Retirement	Good Luck Bob's annual rate of return %	Bad Luck Bob's annual rate of return %
1	34.11	-10.14
2	20.26	-13.04
3	31.01	-23.70
4	26.67	26.38
5	19.53	8.99
6	-10.14	3.00
7	-13.04	13.62
8	-23.7	3.55
9	26.38	-38.47
10	8.99	23.49
11	3.00	12.64
12	13.62	0
13	3.55	13.29
14	-38.47	29.60

15*	23.49	23.50
16*	12.64	23.50
17*	0	23.50
18*	13.29	23.50
19*	29.60	23.50
20*	9.50	23.50
The Result:	Good Luck Bob's nest egg at death: **$2,084,165**	Bad Luck Bob's nest egg at death: **$0**

*Recall that Bad Luck Bob retired in 2000 meaning his 20-year retirement would end with his death in 2020; I use estimates of market returns in years 15 through 20 (2015 through 2020). These years may be unrealistically high but further prove my point: Bad Luck Bob's lousy start hurts him even if the last years of retirement have spectacular returns. In all other years I use Standard & Poor's returns including dividends.

Good Luck Bob and Bad Luck Bob worked hard and saved diligently for retirement. Both accumulated a nice nest egg. Both followed their Wall Street advisor's advice and held on through the market drops. Did Good Luck Bob's Wall Street advisor have any special insider knowledge that a bull market was about to begin? No, not at all (although the advisor may act like he or she did!). Bob was just lucky. Nor did Bad Luck Bob's advisor have any special knowledge about a terrible bear market beginning. Both Wall Street advisors may have meant well. But they are part of a system that has been sold for many years – *a system that tells people like you to stay in stocks as you near retirement and stay in stocks while in retirement.* The system could not be more wrong. And you end up paying the price.

This simple but powerful example illustrates *sequence of return risk.* Wall Street won't explain this to you because it upsets their carefully crafted "buy and hold strategy." Let's be blunt, Bad Luck Bob got screwed. Good Luck Bob's heirs split up the over $2,000,000 that he left behind. Bad Luck Bob's family split up nothing and watched as he struggled to make ends meet during the last years of his life. They may even have pitched in to help him financially.

Sailing into retirement

I've loved sailing all my life. To me, the ocean reminds me of a never ending beautiful cycle with its long waves in the distance and shorter wave forms closer to the shore. It is also cyclical in that storms come and go. But to sail successfully, you have to be ready for both the beautiful sunny days on the ocean as well as the storms that can come up quickly. Wall Street advisors prepare you for those sunny days. But when the storms come, their only advice is to hold on!

Imagine your retirement dream is to own a sail boat. The day you retire the first thing you do is buy your boat. She is beautiful. As soon as you can you test her, setting out with your spouse and friends on a beautiful day sailing the Atlantic. Not a cloud in the sky, your spouse and friends are relaxing; you are at the wheel living your dream. Everything is going great until…in come the clouds. A storm is heading your way.

What should you do? As the water gets rougher and the lightning and thunder begin you call the sail boat salesperson and ask "… what do I do now? Help!" The sales person tells you not to worry. *"After all, statistics are on your side" she tells you – "very few sail boats actually sink. Only 12% of the boats I've sold over the years have sunk. Think of it this way…you, your spouse and your friends have an 88% chance of not drowning in the ocean! Relax, enjoy yourself. Now you just hold on- the storm will eventually pass! Not sure when though, an hour or two, a few days, a week tops. Have a nice day!"*

In this retirement fantasy, the part of the boat salesperson was played by a Wall Street advisor. Notice she didn't guarantee the boat would not sink; she comforted you with a statistic. She didn't even prepare you by telling you what to do to give you a better chance of making it through the storm. "Just hold on…" or was that "just buy and hold?"

In a world of uncertainty, hope for the best, but be prepared for the worst. That is the Common Sense way to prepare for retirement.

No one's retirement should ever be like Bad Luck Bob's. That is why the Common Sense Retirement approach to retirement believes that a retirement plan should have guarantees. I say this to my clients all the time: ***don't buy risk, buy safety.***

Literary Giants on Cycles

"History does not repeat itself, but it does rhyme. It is not worthwhile to try to keep history from repeating itself, for man's character will always make preventing of the repetitions impossible." – Samuel Clemons (Mark Twain)

"Life is just one damn thing after another." – Samuel Clemons (Mark Twain)

"Life isn't just one damn thing after another...it's the same damn thing over and over and over again."
– Edna St. Vincent Millay

What's ahead? Now that you've learned about sequence of return risk, who can you turn to for help? Who can provide you with a retirement plan that addresses your fear of running out of money before running out of breath? Unfortunately, most people turn to Wall Street advisors when seeking a retirement plan. That is the last place you want to go. The truth is that Wall Street does not sell retirement plans. It sells risky investment plans. Wall Street does not have an answer for sequence of return risk. Let's find out why in the next chapter.

CHAPTER THREE

A Boomer's History of Retirement

How you will benefit from reading this chapter: You will better understand Common Sense Retirement if you first understand a little history of retirement planning. By history I mean recent history. You face a much different retirement than your parents did. Fortunately, Common Sense Retirement redefines retirement planning by bringing back some of the best aspects of the retirement your parents enjoyed.

I am one of the almost 76,000,000 million Baby Boomers born between 1945 and 1964. Like the majority of boomers, music has been a big part of my life. Before becoming a financial advisor I was a professional musician. Even now, I still play for audiences. Hearing a song from my teen years can automatically spark good (and occasionally, bad) memories. I'm sure that even now, you can close your eyes and think of a favorite song from those years and remember where you were when you first heard it or remember a special time in your life. Music creates strong emotional memories for most of us.

For example, it has been over 40 years since The Temptations scored a hit single with *Ball of Confusion (That's what the world is today)*. That's right, 40 years. If (like me) you are an older boomer reading this, the song probably popped into your head as soon as you read the title. The lyrics are as true today as they were four decades ago:

So round 'n' round 'n' round we go
Where the world's headed, nobody knows
Just a Ball of Confusion
Oh yea, that's what the world is today

The fact is little has changed in over forty years. The world remains a Ball of Confusion and nobody knows where it's headed. Problems don't disappear, they just change names. Like it or not, that is the world you must prepare to retire in.

One thing, however, remains the same – Wall Street still wants you to believe amidst all this confusion and uncertainty that it has the solution to your quest for a safe, secure retirement.

Wall Street's "solution" to your need for a retirement plan is to sell you an investment plan. In a confusing, uncertain world, Wall Street wants to add to the retirement risks you face. Wall Street is not a solution to the Ball of Confusion; it is part of the problem.

The fact is, Wall Street only makes money if it sells you risk. And that is what an investment plan contains – risk. Oh, Wall Street attempts to disguise or play down risk by using terms and phrases such as "modern portfolio theory," "diversification," "buy and hold," and complicated financial software programs like "Monte Carlo simulations" (a fitting name since Monte Carlo is one of the world's great gambling destinations).

You never hear Wall Street use terms like "guarantee" or "secure."

What if the Wall Street broker or advisor told you he or she could help you design and implement a "risky retirement plan" that may or may not deplete your nest egg before you or your partner died? You would run in the opposite direction!

According to John Bogle, the founder of the Vanguard Group, Wall Street today is nothing more than a "giant Casino." Others have called it a "giant fleecing machine" and guess who is getting fleeced?

Let me ask you this. Why in the world would you ever turn your retirement plan over to a Wall Street broker or advisor who is not interested in selling you a retirement plan?

Common Sense Retirement will provide you the answers you need to create a comfortable, secure retirement.

Can you handle the truth?

Col. Jessup: "You want answers?"
Lt. Kaffee: "I want the truth!"
Col. Jessup: "You can't handle the truth!"

Exchange between Col. Nathan R. Jessup (Jack Nicholson) and Lt. Daniel Kaffee (Tom Cruise) in *A Few Good Men (1992)*

In this book, I will offer you an alternative. I will tell you the truth. Can you handle the truth? I think you can. The Common Sense retirement approach runs counter to what Wall Street and its cheerleaders in the financial press have been telling you for many years. Getting you as far away as I can from the Wall Street casino is a good thing. You will thank me at the end of this book. Hundreds of my clients have a safer, more secure retirement because of my guidance. I want you to benefit from my guidance as well.

Some Historical Perspective

I am a big believer in understanding the history of the stock market and the economy. It may seem strange that I am a historian of the same Wall Street I just happily skewered above. Actually, I am a big fan of the stock market - but only the "up" part – the Bull Market part! I never cared much for the "down" or Bear Market. We'll get to how you can be part of the Bull Market while leaving the Bear Market to others later in the book.

For now, let's take a historical look at how retirement planning has changed over the years. Notice we are not talking about investment planning – we are talking about *retirement planning*. I cannot emphasize enough that these are two entirely separate subjects.

To better understand how we got to where we are, let's go back to 1970.

Ah, 1970.

In 1970 the oldest baby boomers were in their mid-20s. Their *grandparents* were retired; their *parents* looked forward to a comfortable retirement. And why shouldn't their parents who made up the "greatest generation" of World War II be optimistic about retirement? Both Social Security and Medicare appeared financially sound. After all, 76,000,000 Boomers were entering the workforce, all paying into the system that supported the much smaller depression/World War II generations of their parents and grandparents.

To top it off, older workers and their spouses looked forward to a generous pension at age 65. Despite the social strife of the 60s (you know, sex, drugs and rock 'n roll) at least retirement seemed simple enough to plan for. A generous pension, Social Security, Medicare (or, even better, a post-retirement health plan provided by their ex-employer) and a little personal savings meant a comfortable retirement. *You might even call this the "golden age of retirement." But, unfortunately, the golden age of retirement ended in the blink of an eye. Baby boomers live in a different retirement world. This is our challenge – a challenge I think the Common Sense Retirement approach can help you meet.*

Notice what is missing from the discussion of your parent's retirement plan – risk. Social Security and a steady pension would form the most important part of their retirement income. Any savings would be used for "extras" such as a trip to visit grandchildren or take that once in a lifetime dream vacation. Wall Street was still in the early stages of turning safe, secure retirements into a risky gamble with your lifetime savings. Wall Street is a great marketing machine. In this case, Wall Street would sniff out an opportunity – sell middle class families investment services. Scare them into thinking that investing in risky stocks after retirement was the only way they could make their savings last for the rest of their lives. In other words, continue to sell risk, not safety. During the great bull market of 1982 to 2000, Social Security and pensions seemed like relics of a duller, slower time. Some politicians advocated allowing us to "invest" our Social Security contributions into the stock market.

But, Baby Boomers gave little thought to retirement as they began to form households and start families in the 1970s and 1980s.

No one knew what was coming to the world of retirement planning and the transformation that would take place:

- Welcome to the **1970s**. Stagflation, astronomical interest rates, the misery index, a peanut farmer from Georgia becomes president. Coming back to you now?

- The greatest bull market in history kicked off in **1982** and the party didn't stop until **2000**. During that time everyone was an investing genius. In 2000, a famous stock market forecaster predicted a Dow of 40,000 before the coming decade ended. As of this writing, the Dow is still below 20,000.

- The **1980s** saw the decline of the pension plans that Boomer parents enjoyed as they retired. And *overfunded* pensions became the object of corporate takeovers (yes, at one point, many pension funds were considered overfunded – a rare thing nowadays).

- The 401(k) plan was ushered in as the pension plan's replacement and picked up strength as the **1990s** progressed. In light of the great bull market the 401(k) plan was sold as an easy way to wealth for most working Americans. Pensions were abandoned as "old school" retirement planning.

Changes since 1970 meant that the simple world of retirement planning would never be the same. And the Boomers are now bearing the brunt of those changes. But with Common Sense Retirement planning you have the opportunity to go back to a simpler time. A simpler time that worked!

What was happening? The 401(k) and other defined contribution plans work well as *accumulation vehicles*. Over a 25 or 30 year period of saving you can invest contributions into the stock market. You do have the time to "buy and hold" through the ups and downs in the stock market. The 401(k) plan works as a way to accumulate and build your retirement nest egg.

I'll give credit where credit is due – this is where Wall Street got it right – despite the risk, you could accumulate a significant nest egg by investing in stocks. During your accumulation years, working with a good investment advisor paid off. But you are no longer in your accumulation years – you are in your *decumulation* years and you need a new strategy. You need a safe strategy.

Remembering the Boomer Years - *Greed is good*

"The point is ladies and gentlemen that greed, for lack of a better word, is good." Gordon Gekko, *Wall Street* (1987)

Millions of boomers were socking billions of dollars away into the stock market helping to drive the great bull market of 1982 to 2000 (we'll talk in a later chapter about what will happen when the reverse takes place – millions of boomers taking billions of dollars out of the stock market as they retire). Once Wall Street advisors started making big money managing boomer retirement funds did you think they would give it up as boomers turned 50 and needed a better, safer strategy?

Not a chance!

Wall Street merely switched tactics. Wall Street and their cheerleaders in the financial press now wanted you to make your accumulation vehicle into a "decumulation" vehicle keeping a big chunk of your money invested in stocks! In other words, put your retirement nest egg at risk.

Risk with your retirement money? What was unthinkable for your grandparents and your parents was now acceptable for you! As I mentioned above, Wall Street learned to supposedly minimize the "risk" it was selling you by coming up with fancy theories (portfolio theory, optimization, diversification and on and on) and complicated algorithms (the Monte Carlo simulation and "quantitative" investment approaches developed by academic eggheads). At least it sounded good. The so-called "quants" turned Wall Street on its head – look at the history of the 1987 crash (thank you, portfolio insurance which was blamed for the crash) and the more recent "flash crash" in 2010 and the tremendous overall increase in stock market volatility. And that is where many investment advisors want you to put your retirement nest egg.

In other words, at the exact same time the stock market was becoming even less safe for your retirement nest egg; many advisors began selling you on the need to keep invested in stocks! According to these advisors you need a risky investment plan if you hope to make your nest egg last.

Now the really painful part began. The "dot com crash" woke us all up in 2000 – but many of us didn't learn a thing from that. And that refusal to learn set many investors up for the **2008** real estate and credit market collapse. By the way, with that crash, modern "portfolio theory" also took a hit. The academics that developed that theory were left (appropriately) with egg on their face. What you heard from them was "it wasn't supposed to happen like that" as all stock portfolio asset classes fell at the same time.

In 2008 there was no place to hide. For many retirees whatever they had left after the dot com crash was finished off with the credit/real estate crash.

I hope my little history lesson here demonstrates that the changes since 1970 meant that the simple world of retirement planning would never be the same.

Remembering the Boomer Years – this is not your father's Oldsmobile

In what turned out to be an unsuccessful effort to save its Oldsmobile brand, GM ran a series of ads in the late 1980s trying to convince boomers to take a look at the new Olds – it was not "your father's Oldsmobile." Well, the new retirement is neither your father's nor your mother's retirement. As of this writing, plans are underway to convince the Gen-Xers that Buick is not their father's Buick. Feeling old?

What history teaches us

I think history should teach us humility.

No one can consistently predict the great things in store for us.

On April 3, 1973, in front of a group of reporters, a manager at Motorola placed a cellular phone call to a scientist at Bell Labs. The rest, as they say, is history. But who knew where that simple test call would lead? Now most of us (and our kids and grandkids) own cellular smart phones that fit in our pocket. A whole new industry was created.

No one can consistently predict the terrible things in store for us.

A famous prognosticator predicted the Dow Jones would hit 40,000 in just a few years. His prediction was made just before the dot com crash of 2000. But he was not alone. The fact is the person who makes the right call – even if it is the only correct call he or she will ever make – has all the incentive in the world to trumpet his or her achievement over and over again. He or she becomes the great guru – at least until they make a wrong prediction (which they always do). At the same time, the forecasters who get it wrong go silent. Until by chance, they get it right. And then they never shut up.

The fact is, investment advisors cannot predict the future, never could, never will.

We live in an uncertain world with unprecedented challenges ahead of us.

Common sense tells us that the only way to plan for uncertain times is by structuring your retirement plan around guarantees. You need a guaranteed source of growing income and protection of your retirement nest egg. The world still is a Ball of Confusion. And the band plays on. Seek certainty in an uncertain world. I will show you how in the pages that follow.

Not Just for Boomers

You are a Boomer if you were born *between* 1945 and 1965 (in other words, in 1946 through 1964). There are 76,000,000 of us. This book, however, is for non-boomers as well as the boomers.

If you were born before 1946, you are not a considered a Boomer. However, just because the vast majority of those born before 1946 are age 70 or older, doesn't mean the planning ideas in this book don't apply to you. In fact, it may be more important for you to read this book than it is for boomers! You also may be married to a boomer, so read this book together.

If you were born after 1964, you are not a boomer but the oldest of you turned 50 in 2014! You have a great advantage…you are at the exact right age to get the most benefit from this book. Read on!

What's ahead? No one can predict the future. I know I cannot. Many investment advisors claim they can buy and sell stocks and do better than the stock market overall. But very few can beat the overall stock market consistently. They may do well over a period of years, but ultimately they fall back to the pack. Even if some active managers could beat the overall stock market, there is no sure fire way of picking that manager. As an alternative, many knowledgeable investors recommend you invest in a stock market index. A stock market index is a simple concept – it purchases all the stocks in an index. For example, the Standard and Poor's 500 or the Dow Jones Industrial Average. Being a "passive" investor has one big advantage – it is a cheaper way to invest. In the next chapter I'll describe why index investing makes sense and how it fits in Common Sense Retirement.

CHAPTER FOUR

Stock Indexes and Common Sense Retirement Planning

How you will benefit from reading this chapter: By reading this chapter on stock market indexes you will get closer to understanding how Common Sense Retirement Planning will help you build a secure retirement that guarantees that you will not run out of money before running out of breath! Stock indexes are a measuring tool used to compute the gains in your secure retirement nest egg. These gains can increase both the value of your nest egg and the income paid to you from the account. If the stock market index suffers losses in a year don't worry – your account will see none of the loss. So, read on!

Stock market indexes have a special (although indirect) role to play in Common Sense Retirement Planning. Remember, Common Sense Retirement Planning is about *retirement planning* – it is not about investment planning. A little later in this book you will learn about secure retirement products that use *stock market indexes* as a measuring tool to determine how much annual gain you made in the value of your nest egg or the increase in your income stream. You will learn that in these products you will benefit from an up year in the stock market and lock in the gain. But if the stock market goes down, your account value will not go down with it. Remember I wrote earlier that I love the stock market – but just the up part, not the down part? When you read that you probably asked yourself "how can you benefit just from the upside of the stock market? I thought you had to take the bad with the good." You'll get closer to understanding what I mean by learning a little bit about stock market indexes.

In the United States alone, there are almost 5,000 individual stocks an investor may select from to build his or her portfolio. Add to that the thousands of individual stocks from around the world and you can begin to understand how difficult it is to find a few good stocks to invest in. Even if you have the interest and inclination, the time it takes to evaluate or "screen" all the available stocks to find the proverbial needle in a haystack is prohibitive.

Let's face it, few of us have the time, interest or discipline to study and invest in the individual stocks we may find attractive.

OK, you don't have the time or inclination to find individual stocks to invest in. What about finding a few good mutual funds to invest in? After all, why not let experts with a staff of researchers scour the world over to find the best stocks to invest in?

Well first, in the U.S. there are thousands of mutual funds to choose from. It seems at times that there are as many mutual funds as there are U.S. stocks to choose from! That puts us back where we started – do you have the time to study which mutual fund (or mutual funds if you build a portfolio of several funds) to invest in? What criteria will you use to select a "good" fund? Many mutual fund investors will chase after the most recent best performers – the ones they hear about in the popular financial press or on TV. These individuals invest their money in last year's "hot fund" just as the fund cools and lags behind its competitors. Every year a new financial "genius" appears and is hyped in the press only to crash and burn later. Most of the investors who bought the fund bought it at the top – and ride it to the bottom!

Another problem is cost; all that research conducted by the mutual fund manager is not free. Many mutual funds charge **1% or more** of each dollar you invest with them to cover the costs of research. There are plenty of other administrative and trading costs involved with running a mutual fund that must be covered. All these costs do one thing – eat into the return you will receive from your investments.

The fact is the stock market is so competitive that it is difficult for an *active* investment manager to do better than the stock market as a whole. Notice I threw in the word *active* meaning a manager who *actively seeks* out the best investment opportunities from the many thousands of individual stocks that are available.

Many years ago, some academics began to wonder if the costs of active management are worth it. Why not, they wondered, just invest in the stock market as a whole? The overall trend of the market is up and if you can stand the downturns in the market and stay invested over the long term you will probably do better than most active managers. And you'll save on the costs of active management. (If part of this sounds familiar, it is the "buy and hold" approach we discussed – and debunked – earlier in the book). This investment approach is referred to as **"passive investing"** since it does not rely on active management.

As a practical matter it is difficult for a small investor to buy the "whole market." In fact, when the passive investing idea started to catch on in the mid-1970s, buying the market was available only through a mutual fund company named Vanguard. Its founder, John Bogle, was a passionate believer in passive investing. He left the investment company he was working with to found Vanguard. Bogle will tell you that the first passive investment fund was not created at Vanguard but at Wells Fargo Bank. Be that as it may, Bogle is the most responsible for popularizing the idea among consumers.

The first fund created was the Vanguard 500 Index Fund Investor Shares on August 31, 1976. This passive fund does not invest in the whole market. It invests in an index – the Standard & Poor's 500 (or S&P 500). The S&P 500 is made up of 500 large company stocks. Standard and Poor's decides which stocks will be included in the index. Sometimes stocks are dropped while others are added.

Lots of Indexes to Choose From

There are many different types of indexes for a passive investor to choose from. There are:

- Global indexes
- Regional (e.g., Asia, Europe)
- National (e.g., Denmark, Indonesia, the United States)
- Indexes based on either small, mid-sized, large companies (usually based on annual sales)
- Industry (e.g., finance, clean energy)

In addition to stock indexes, there are also *bond indexes* that work much the same way.

Here is the connection between passive investing and indexes. There are a lot of different stock market indexes. In addition to the S&P 500 there is the Dow Jones Industrial Average. Dow Jones, the publisher of the Wall Street Journal, decides which companies (usually very large companies!) will go into its index. While the S&P index has 500 companies, the Dow Jones Industrial Average has only 30 companies.

The stocks that make up the S&P and the Dow Jones index are not determined based on performance. They are included in the indexes because the owner of the index believes the companies included represent an important segment of the market. When a mutual fund is established using the index, it invests only in the companies that make up the index (if it varies from the index at all, it must let investors know).

As I just described, there are many different stock indexes that can be used. There are stock indexes that cover only small companies in the United States or small companies abroad. There are stock indexes that cover only mid-sized companies or companies in certain industries (such as utilities or transportation). If you can think of a stock market segment there is usually an index that covers it. There are indexes geared toward the socially conscious investor and, at the other end of the spectrum, an index based on the seven deadly sins! And yes, there is a mutual fund that uses the seven deadly sins index! Wall Street always knows how to exploit a marketing opportunity.

Seven Deadly Sins?

I know you are curious about the index based on the seven deadly sins! The types of companies and industries that make up the index include:

- Gluttony – fast food, smoking
- Sloth – cable TV
- Greed – Wall Street firms
- Envy – gambling
- Vanity – cosmetics
- Wrath – gun manufacturers
- Lust – lingerie companies

Some would argue that this is not an index in the strictest sense of the term but if you want to make money off the weaknesses of your fellow human beings, this is the place to go.

But don't let the silliness of a seven deadly sins index make you lose focus on the importance of passive investing and low cost index funds.

My point is this: passive investing is a low cost way of investing in the stock market. Passive investing uses indexes to determine which stocks will be in its portfolio. If the index drops or adds a stock, the mutual fund will do the same so it continues to match or "track" the index. With passive investing, there is no active management and its associated costs. For example, the annual cost of the Vanguard 500 fund is just 17 cents per hundred dollars invested. Many active managed funds charge $1.50 to $2.50 per hundred dollars invested! Those extra costs add up and can reduce your return over a long period of time by 50%.

For our purposes, you will learn later that the indexes are used merely as a tool to measure the gains you will recognize in your secure retirement nest egg. You don't actually invest your money in a stock market index with these products.

Do the indexes outperform the active managers?

Studies consistently show that a good majority of actively managed mutual funds do not perform as well as passively managed mutual funds. Part of this is due to cost – the active manager must overcome higher costs than, say the Vanguard 500 Index Fund. Even if the actively managed fund and the Vanguard 500 fund annual return is the same, the Vanguard cost advantage means the index fund will win. If the annual cost in the actively managed fund is 2% and the Vanguard cost is .17%; the active manager must outperform the index fund by 1.83% just to break even!

What's ahead? *Next we will take a closer look at the 4% "rule of thumb." The 4% rule of thumb has been around for a long time. It seems simple enough and promises that if followed your chances of outliving your money are small. But in the next chapter we'll go back to the sequence of return risk I introduced to you in Chapter 1 and see how your retirement portfolio can be devastated when you follow the 4% rule based on an advisor's recommendation and retire at the wrong time. It is time to revisit Good Luck Bob and Bad Luck Bob.*

CHAPTER FIVE

The 4% Rule Meets the Real World

How you will benefit from reading this chapter: You will learn what to avoid – simplistic rules of thumb that can cause you to run out of money long before you run out of breath. Learn to question everything you hear about retirement planning!

The financial planning world is made up of dozens of rules of thumb, some good, some bad, some downright dangerous. Here are two that, when combined, can decimate your nest egg before you die:

- The stock market has a long-term average annual return of 10%.

- You can withdraw 4% of your retirement nest egg annually, plus an adjustment for inflation, and have a good chance that you will not run out of money before you die.

Let's take a close look at these two rules of thumb.

The stock market has a long-term average return of 10% - the key word here is "average." Whether the stock market has a long term average annual return of 10% is beside the point. In the real world, the 10% annual return includes some years of steep, heart-stopping drops, some years of exhilarating increases and a lot of so-so years. Unfortunately, many investment advisors use this average return as an argument for staying in stocks after retirement. Think back to Chapter 2 - you met Good Luck Bob and Bad Luck Bob. ***Both earned the same long term rate of return on their retirement nest egg.*** But Good Luck Bob retired at the beginning of a bull (up) market. Bad Luck Bob retired at the beginning of a long-term bear (down) market. The same long-term average returns but Good Luck Bob died with a large nest egg after living the type of retirement he dreamed of. Bad Luck Bob ran out of money before he died.

It is worth repeating again and again, ***both earned the same long term rate of return on their retirement nest egg but experienced very different results.***

You can withdraw 4% of your retirement nest egg annually, adjust the withdrawal for inflation and have a very good chance of not running out of money before you die – not if you are Bad Luck Bob!

Believing the Impossible

"I try to believe in as many as six impossible things before breakfast. Count them, Alice. One, there are drinks that make you shrink. Two, there are foods that make you grow. Three, animals can talk. Four, cats can disappear. Five, there is a place called Underland. Six, I can slay the Jabberwocky."
— Lewis Carroll, *Alice in Wonderland*

And let me add a seventh – you can withdraw 4% of your nest egg each year and never run out of money!

Here's the problem with the 4% rule of thumb – it just does not work in the world! Let's look at an example that will prove my point. In the first table, the retiree owns a $100,000 nest egg. The 4% rule states that she can withdraw $4,000 each year with an adjustment for inflation. In year one, she withdraws $4,000 or $100,000 times 4% at the beginning of the year. During the year, inflation was 3%. In year two, she withdraws $4,000 plus $120 to keep up with inflation ($4,000 times 3% is $120; $4,000 plus $120 equals $4,120). Earnings on the account are a smooth 4.5% each year. With a smooth rate of return, the retiree makes her withdrawals each year, plus inflation and her nest egg has actually grown at the end of four years. Her balance is $101,297.

Rather than get caught up in all the numbers, look at the charts below.

The 4% Rule of Thumb in a Perfect World

Year	Beginning Balance	4% Annual Distribution Set in Year 1	Annual Inflation Adjustment	Inflation Adj. W/D @ Beg. Of Yr.	Earnings @4.5%*	Year End Balance
1	$100,000	$4,000	n/a	($4,000)	$4,500	$100,500
2	$100,320	$4,000	3%	($4,120)	$4,523	$100,903
3	$100,529	$4,000	3.5%	($4,264)	$4,541	$101,179
4	$100,727	$4,000	4.0%	($4,435)	$4,553	$101,297

The 4% rule assumes withdrawals begin at age 65 and the retirement

---

Common Sense Retirement

nest egg is invested 60% in large cap stocks; 40% in bonds.
<u>**Where did the 4% Rule of Thumb come from?**</u>

The 4% rule of thumb was originally the brain child of a financial planner named Bill Bengen. He was a real number cruncher. Bengen studied every 30-year period (roughly the length of a long retirement) beginning in 1926 through 1955. In other words, the first retirement period studied was 1926 through 1955; the last period studied was 1955 through 1984. In all, 30 periods were studied. The purpose was to discover how much could be withdrawn from a portfolio without running out of money. Based on his study, Bengen determined that a withdrawal rate of 4.15% with adjustments for inflation could be sustained for at least 30 years. But Bengen did not *guarantee* that the portfolio would last 30 years.

Despite Bengen's impressive work, other financial planners and academics wondered "what if annual earnings were not a smooth 4.5% per year?" After all, that never happens in real life. Remember our discussion regarding cycles in Chapter Two? Let's go back to the annual returns Bad Luck Bob suffered in just his first four years of retirement.

The 4% Rule of Thumb in the Real World

Year	Beginning Balance	4% Annual Distribution Set in Year 1	Annual Inflation Adjustment	Inflation Adj. W/D @ Beg. Of Yr.	Earnings	Year End Balance
1	$100,000	$4,000	n/a	($4,000)	-.221	$73,900
2	$73,900	$4,000	3%	($4,120)	-.1181	$61,052
3	$61,052	$4,000	3.5%	($4,140)	-.0911	$51,226
4	$51,226	$4,000	4.0%	($4,160)	+.2104	$57,570

Compare the idealized 4% withdrawal rule balance at the end of year 4 or <u>$101,297</u> to the real world sequence of return risk balance at the end of year 4 or <u>$57,570</u>. This is a difference of <u>$43,727</u>. Illustrating the sequence of return risk shows that retiring into a bear market while still maintaining the planned 4% (plus inflation) withdrawal will devastate the portfolio. As a result, the portfolio may be fully depleted years before otherwise planned.

Of course, Bad Luck Bob most likely would have thrown in the towel on his stock market investments well before the end of year 4. Who would blame him? For almost all retirees, their tolerance for risk goes down in retirement. At some point, whether at the end of year 1 or year 3 he may sell his stock holdings and move his remaining funds into a cash account. Bad Luck Bob will sit on the sidelines until the stock market has a few good years. At that point, he will confidently plunge back into the market - just in time to catch the next market drop.

Want a more recent real life example? From mid-2007 to mid-2009, the S&P 500 declined by 52.4% (the price per share of the Vanguard S&P Fund was $142.83 at its peak; two years later the price per share was $67.99). Bad Luck Bob would have become the poster boy for bad timing. His stock portfolio would have dropped from $100,000 to approximately $40,000. All of his retirement expectations would be gone in just his first two years of retirement. With the Common Sense Retirement Plan that would have never happened.

More and more planners as well as reporters in the popular financial press began focusing on the weakness of the 4% rule. Consider recent headlines:

"Say Goodbye to the 4% Rule"
(The Wall Street Journal)
"Forget the 4% withdrawal rule"
(CNN Money)
"Rethinking the 4% retirement spending rule"
(The Wall Street Journal)

In addition, new studies confirmed the weakness of the 4% rule when an individual has the misfortune, like Bad Luck Bob, to retire at the onset of a bear market. For example, there is an often cited study by T. Rowe Price, the large mutual fund company. It showed that if you retired at the onset of a bear market, the chances of your portfolio lasting for thirty years decreased to only 29%! That means a 71% chance of failure! And that means living out your golden years on Social Security and your pension (if you are lucky enough to have a pension). For confirmation, revisit the table entitled "The 4% Rule of Thumb in the Real World."

What went wrong?

In order to work, the 4% rule requires strong stock and bond returns to "refresh" your portfolio after you make your annual withdrawal. The first strike against the 4% rule was an individual retiring into the teeth of a bear market. Even when the market subsequently goes up, the returns are not sufficient to fully "refresh" your portfolio – *your losses are permanent.* The second strike is a prolonged down cycle (revisit the discussion in Chapter Two on cycles) in the stock market. Prolonged down cycles never allow you to regain your losses. Recovery is impossible.

The final strike is a prolonged period of low interest rates. *When interest rates are low, it is the savers and those who live off interest who suffer.* In the past few years (since the Great Recession) the Federal Reserve has made a concerted effort to keep interest rates at historically low levels. Some commentators call this "financial repression" which forces savers to move from historically safe savings accounts, CDs, Treasury Bills, etc. into riskier, more volatile assets such as stocks if they hope to realize any gain in their portfolio at all. We will return to this topic in subsequent chapters.

But where are the guarantees?

There are dozens of articles offering variations on the 4% rule to increase the likelihood of your portfolio lasting 30 years. In addition, there is no end to the financial planners and academics that have proposed alternative withdrawal strategies to the 4% rule.

But none of these approaches, whether fine-tuning this popular rule of thumb or proposing whole new strategies, make any guarantees. Think about how long it took for the inherent weakness in the 4% rule to be discovered and debunked. How many retirees following the rule saw their portfolios depleted and their retirement ruined? Will your advisor have you adopt a strategy that may eventually be debunked after a huge market drop finally exposes its weaknesses?

With the Common Sense Retirement plan you lock in your income stream with guarantees. It does not depend on the latest academic research and theories or the expert opinion of a financial planner.

What's ahead? In the next chapter we will look at what has been called the "new normal" of the U.S. economy since the Great Recession. The fact is it is not the "little guy" (or gal) who got the benefit of the U.S. government bailout of our financial system. The banks and Wall Street benefited while the U.S. taxpayer footed the bill. The consequences and cost of the bailout have not yet run their course. In addition to the changes caused by the bailout, we will look at other factors – such as an aging worldwide population – that require you take a different approach – The Common Sense Retirement approach – to planning for your future.

CHAPTER SIX

Hoping for the Best,
Planning for the Worst

How you will benefit from reading this chapter: *Investing in the stock market has always been a risky proposition. The changes we have seen since the Great Recession, however, have been unprecedented and have increased the risk many times. Maybe this time, things are truly different. In this chapter we discuss the debt super cycle and how the enormous debt built up by the U.S. government since the onset of the Great Recession means Common Sense Retirement planning is needed more than ever. You'll learn who benefited the most from U.S. government bailouts (spoiler alert – it wasn't you or me!).*

In late 2008 the growth in U.S. government debt began to exceed the growth in household and business debt. In other words, as the financial crisis that began in August of 2007 deepened, U.S. households and corporations began paying back their debts. In response to the slowing growth of private debt, the U.S. government began to substantially increase *its* level of debt.

Here is the ultimate three shell game played by Wall Street, the big banks and the U.S. government. The debts under the household debt shell and business debt shell were simply moved to the government debt shell.

Remember the refrain from The Temptations' 1970 song "Ball of Confusion" that I mentioned in Chapter 3? Well, when it comes to debt "…the band played on." To keep the economy moving along, debt was just moved around. Debt buildup has gone from businesses and consumers to the U.S. government. The problem is – when the bond market suddenly refuses to buy U.S. government bonds, what next?

Since the onset of the Great Recession, the Federal Reserve has kept interest rates historically low, offering no alternative for savers and retirees other than to put their money into the stock market. Earning less than one-half percent on a CD just won't cut it for retirees and other conservative investors. This has created a bull market in stocks that cannot continue. Stock prices have increased not because of the underlying value and economic prospects of the company but because of the Federal Reserve policy of keeping interest rates low. Of course, no one complains as the stock market hits new "highs" (although, on an inflation adjusted basis, these new "highs" are anything but impressive!).

There will be a day of reckoning. This debt buildup will only continue until the bond market says "enough" and refuses to buy more debt from Uncle Sam. Or the bond market will require much higher interest rates on U.S. government obligations. This all will end in a bang, not a whimper.

The question is: where do you want to be at the end? I cannot tell you when this will end, but I can warn you that it will end. Interest rates will spike, bond prices will collapse. The stock market will crash (again) and when it does, the recovery may well take years, even decades.

The coming calamity is the reason I could not sit by and watch so many lose so much. It is the reason I developed the Common Sense Retirement planning program. Recall, in the introduction I discussed how many people today plan for retirement without heeding the obvious warning signs. It is as if they are traveling on a road going 90 miles an hour and ignore signs reading: WARNING! DANGEROUS CONDITIONS AHEAD! In fact, many of my fellow baby boomers are going even faster, taking on more and more risk in their retirement plan. Consider the Common Sense Retirement plan as your warning sign and your protection from the dangerous conditions ahead.

Origins of the Great Recession

What some have called the **debt super cycle** had come to an end in 2007.

Since 1992, private debt (meaning debt taken on by consumers and private businesses) had increased to unsustainable levels. This is best illustrated by home mortgages. More individuals and families qualified for mortgages than ever before. In truth, many of these individuals and families should not have qualified for the mortgages they received. Recall the prevailing wisdom of the time? "Buy more house than you can afford! Home prices just keep going up." Seems laughable now, doesn't it?

The banks, aided and abetted by the Federal government, loaned money to millions of unqualified borrowers. In the face of unprecedented demand fueled by easy mortgage terms, home prices continued to increase. When home prices crashed, the borrowers were "upside down," meaning the debt on their homes exceeded the value of their home. With the economic slowdown and job losses, millions of families could no longer meet their mortgage obligations. Home foreclosures reached epidemic levels and the lenders found themselves with a growing inventory of homes and worthless mortgages.

To make matters worse, millions of mortgages were sold ("securitized") so that investors could invest in pools of mortgages, a move that supposedly reduced their risk while allowing them to earn a better rate of return. When home prices crashed, there was no place to hide! These pools contained thousands of very risky mortgages. The problem was, the originators of the loans were able to sell the loans to these pools. What did the bank care if the loan was risky or they were sloppy in applying strict lending standards? Once the loan was sold it was someone else's problem!

Of course, it would be simplistic to blame the Great Recession on home mortgages alone. Add to that the "shadow banking system." Shadow banks were not really banks, and therefore not subject to government banking regulations. Unlike banks, shadow banks did not have to maintain a reserve against their loans. There was no cushion when borrowers defaulted. As a result, shadow banks collapsed quickly, taking depositors and shareholders with them. The most famous of these was Lehman Brothers.

...and the band played on.

The *Federal Reserve* stepped in to buy the defaulting mortgage bonds to prevent a collapse of the U.S. mortgage market.

The *Federal Government* stepped in to make up for the shrinking private debt market as consumers and businesses paid back their debt by massively increasing its borrowing. Bailouts of financial institutions began – they were "too big to fail" we were told. This cost taxpayers billions. "Stimulus packages" were passed that added trillions to the national debt.

And that is how we got to the point in late 2008 when U.S. government borrowing began growing faster than private borrowing.

Add to the growing U.S. government debt the entitlement debt – Social Security, Medicare and Medicaid promises we have made to millions of fellow citizens (mostly Baby Boomers born between 1945 and 1965) and we have debts that cannot be paid off. At this point, I could give you the figures (for example, future Medicare promises will cost in the range of $50 to $100 trillion depending on the assumptions used!) of indebtedness but these numbers are, to me, meaningless to average people like you and me. Let me put it this way, the U.S. economy is valued at almost *$15 trillion* dollars. We owe more than three to six times the size of our whole economy in just Medicare promises alone!

To meet these obligations (if, in fact, we are able to do so) the tax increases will have to be enormous. These tax increases will not just impact the generations that follow the Baby Boomers, but will also impact Boomers!

Questions: Will the generations following us be willing to pay the increased taxes that will be demanded? We can only hope so.

If the U.S. government cannot fulfill its promises under Social Security, Medicare and Medicaid or even if there is just a chance these promises cannot be fulfilled, *shouldn't your retirement plan prepare you for the worst while you hope for the best?*

That is what the Common Sense Retirement plan does.

The War on Retirees and Savers

As house prices collapsed so did the stock and bond market. Recall that the stock market lost over 50% of its value during the Great Recession. The bond market also collapsed over the fear of business borrowers being unable to repay their debt. So much for the long held beliefs that diversification brought safety. No one was safe; there was no place to hide.

The Federal Reserve moved quickly to save the big banks. It imposed "quantitative easing," or QE, as a way to keep interest rates low.

Borrowers generally applaud low interest rates – it lowers the cost of their debt. But what about retirees and savers who depend on higher interest rates? The fact is retirees and savers are the ones that pay the price. Retirees live off their savings. When CDs were paying the now unheard of rates of 5% or higher, retirees could afford to live off their savings. That is not true when interest rates are well under 1%. At that rate seniors have to consume their nest eggs and hope they don't run out of money before running out of breath.

Savers also suffer for the same reason – very low interest rates do not offer an attractive rate of return. What do retirees and savers do?

As discussed above, savers and retirees had only one alternative to interest rates below one-half percent - invest in riskier assets – they must turn to the stock market to achieve any type of decent return. Of course, the Federal Reserve knows this. As more money pours into the stock market, stock prices go up – if for no other reason than the increase in demand as retirees and savers seek greater returns.

What happened? Savers and retirees are being asked to bail out the bad economic actors who brought us the Great Recession. And what happens when the stock market collapses again as stock prices are driven to unreasonable heights? Ah, well, we'll deal with that problem when the time comes.

Don't you see what is going on here? Everyone is bailed out but the saver and the retiree. Your prudent financial behavior goes unrewarded. In fact, your good behavior is punished while the bad economic actors are "bailed out" because they are "too big to fail." Wall Street and the big banks made out like bandits (and I mean that literally!).

Wall Street is Not the Economy

One more thing before we move on. Often an up stock market is confused for a growing economy. That is not always the case. It is possible to have a growing economy while the stock market is taking a hit and have an up market while the economy is slowing or in a recession. I always take the time to educate my clients about their personal finances in the context of a much broader economy. I teach them to look beneath the obvious to get a real sense of what is going on.

In the past few years we've seen just that, with stock market performance bearing no resemblance to the overall economy. We've had an almost non-existent recovery since the Great Recession. Inflation is reportedly low, but you know the truth when you stop at the gas station or visit the grocery store. Unemployment goes down only because so many of us have left the job market – a sad commentary that many of our fellow citizens have given up hope of ever finding employment.

What does all this mean to your Retirement Plan?

Uncertain times are not new. Remember Ecclesiastes 1:9 (KJV).

⁹ The thing that hath been, it is that which shall be; and that which is done is that which shall be done: and there is no new thing under the sun.

But the amount of debt taken on by the U.S. government (and governments around the world) is unprecedented (except in times of war). At the same time, we are facing demographic changes as 10,000 Baby Boomers on average turn age 65 every day. The generations behind the Boomers have had fewer and fewer children. This means that while in 1960 there were five workers to every Social Security eligible beneficiary, in 2030 (just 16 years from the time this book is being written) there will be just two workers for every Social Security eligible beneficiary.

No one is facing these facts – except you and me! To make matters worse, these problems are worldwide. With Common Sense Retirement planning you can build a fortress around your retirement plan, protecting your plan from worldwide risks. Before we explain how you can do that, we'll take a look at some worldwide problems that also stand between you and a safe, secure retirement.

What's ahead? *In the next chapter, I present my Common Sense Retirement tool.*

CHAPTER SEVEN

Fixed Index Annuities

How you will benefit from reading this chapter: *In this chapter I bring it all together for you. There is a solution to all the retirement issues and problems I discussed in the first six chapters. It is what I refer to as the Common Sense Retirement Tool. I would never recommend something I would not use myself. I've benefited from this retirement tool as have hundreds of my clients. Most of you reading this book have either (i) never heard of this tool or (ii) heard only half-truths and misrepresentations that may have closed your mind to my Common Sense Retirement Tool. The focus of this chapter is on a new type of annuity. Why? The title of my book's Introduction says it all: Income is the Right Outcome. For Boomers close to retirement or already retired, their accumulating years are over. They must now focus on holding on to what they have and – at the same time – look for a way create a dependable, growing stream of income that will last a lifetime for them and their partner. This income must be generated from the assets they've worked so hard to accumulate. I promise you, after reading this chapter, you will never think about retirement planning the same again and you will share my optimism and excitement that there is a better solution.*

I've spent a great deal of time explaining the economic environment and the risks facing those nearing retirement or already retired. Let me tell you why so much time has been spent on these issues.

Imagine you are planning to hike into the depths of the Amazon rainforest. A wise, experienced hiker would do a great deal of research on the nature of the Amazon environment and prepare for the numerous dangers that are ahead. Our brave hiker would want to be aware of the ravenous wild animals, poisonous insects and diseases. The hiker would include essential items in his or her backpack such as water purification filters, mosquito netting, a knife, machete, matches, rain gear, sleeping bag, tent, compass, and (just maybe) a firearm. No experienced hiker would attempt such a trek unprepared.

I believe retirement is similar to a long hike; you must be prepared for what is ahead. For that reason, I believe it is essential to lay out the true dangers that can derail your retirement. That is exactly what I have done in the first six chapters of my book. Once those dangers are understood, you can prepare properly for what should be a wonderful time in your life. Retirement is a 20 to 30 year (or more) trek. The dangers may be less than a hike through the Amazon rainforest, but are no less daunting. For your retirement trek, there is a tool that is absolutely essential to your safety. I call it the Common Sense Retirement Tool. It belongs in every retiree's backpack.

So now, let us turn our attention from the Amazon rainforest to retirement planning and the value of zero. Yes, zero has tremendous value!

The Value of Zero

In Chapter Two, I introduced you to Good Luck Bob and Bad Luck Bob. Good Luck Bob had the fortune to retire with $1,000,000 in his retirement nest egg just at the beginning of a great Bull Market. Thanks to his timing, he was able to withdraw $50,000 per year from his nest egg (adjusted annually for inflation) for 20 years. When he died, he was able to pass on to his family and his charitable causes almost $2,000,000. His $1,000,000 nest egg produced over $1,300,000 in cash distributions and a $2,000,000 legacy, or $3,300,000 in all.

Bad Luck Bob retired with a $1,000,000 nest egg and also withdrew $50,000 per year (adjusted annually for inflation). Unfortunately, Bad Luck Bob retired into a Bear Market. Overall, his returns were the same as Good Luck Bob but just reversed (see the table below). While Good Luck Bob's first three years in retirement had terrific returns and were able to support his income withdrawals, Bad Luck Bob's first three years in retirement realized horrific returns that, in combination with his annual withdraws, devastated his portfolio. Bad Luck Bob's nest egg ran out several years before he died.

Review Bad Luck Bob's annual returns below. You'll notice that his "bad luck" consisted of just five years of losses over 20 years. Unfortunately, the worst of the losses came in his first three years of retirement. His name might better be Bad Timing Bob. Bad Luck Bob was a victim of the sequence of return risk I outlined in Chapter Two.

Now let me introduce you to Common Sense Retirement Bob. His total returns over the twenty years were exactly the same as Bad Luck Bob (both had average annual returns of 9.51%). There is one big difference – instead of having four down years, I turned the returns in those years to zero for Common Sense Retirement Bob. Now, Common Sense Retirement Bob is able to withdraw the inflation-adjusted $50,000 per year and at his death he also was able to leave a legacy of $834,541! He did this without suffering through the down markets that Bad Luck and Good Luck Bob had endured. When you consider that Common Sense Retirement Bob was able to leave a legacy while taking on much less risk than both Bad Luck Bob and Good Luck Bob, you can appreciate the value of the Common Sense Retirement Tool.

We saw earlier how negative market returns devastated Bad Luck Bob's nest egg. Let's look at how Common Sense Retirement Bob did during the same market years using the Common Sense Retirement Tool:

Year of Retirement	Bad Luck Bob's annual rate of return %	Common Sense Retirement Bob's annual rate of return % with a Fixed Index Annuity (55% participation rate)
1	-10.14	0
2	-13.04	0
3	-23.70	0
4	26.38	14.51
5	8.99	4.94
6	3.00	1.65
7	13.62	7.49
8	3.55	1.95
9	-38.47	0
10	23.49	12.92
11	12.64	6.95
12	0	0
13	13.29	7.31
14	29.60	16.28
15*	23.50	12.93
16*	23.50	12.93
17*	23.50	12.93
18*	23.50	12.93
19*	23.50	12.93
20*	23.50	12.93
The Result	Bad Luck Bob's nest egg at death: $0	Common Sense Retirement Bob's nest egg at death: $834,541

*Recall that Bad Luck Bob retired in 2000 meaning his twenty year retirement would end with his death in 2020; I use estimates of market returns in years 15 through 20 (2015 through 2020). These numbers were chosen that the total returns earned by both Good Luck Bob and Common Sense Retirement Bob *were the same (9.51%). This is so we can compare apples to apples. These years may be unrealistically high but are offset by the 55% participation rate.*

How can I help you do this?

I help you accomplish this with inflation-adjusted Fixed Index Annuities (FIAs) – my *Common Sense Retirement Tool.* Look at the last column in the above table. Common Sense Retirement Bob realized none of the down years – in those years his portfolio did not go down. In the up years, he realized 55% of the gain in the index.

The FIA is the Common Sense Retirement Tool – because it allows you to *capture some of the upside of the stock market but none of the downside.* This exact same approach during your retirement years can also provide you with a dependable stream of growing lifetime income without having to surrender your nest egg and leave your beneficiaries with nothing.

Even though Good Luck Bob (who, remember, was lucky in his sequence of returns) ended up with a larger nest egg than Common Sense Retirement Bob, keep in mind that Good Luck Bob might have gotten out of the market during his downturn years (years 6-8). He may have never returned after that, or perhaps returned only several years later, thereby missing out on the recovery years that started in his 9th year of retirement. This is why the psychological aspects of investing cannot be ignored, especially during retirement when we are all especially sensitive to stock market losses!

The greatest story *never* told (or at least never *properly* told!)

Uh-oh - I can already see you recoiling. "Did he just use the "A" word?" Yep, he did. Before you close the book because you've heard that annuities are bad, *let me agree with you that a lot of annuities are bad.* Many older annuities are outdated and unsuitable for the current world of retirement.

Do you have an Uncle Henry?

Everyone has an Uncle Henry who thinks he knows everything and has the answer to every problem. And he isn't shy about sharing his knowledge and giving advice – even if the knowledge is out of date or just plain wrong. We all have an "Uncle Henry" in our life. Of course, it doesn't have to be an uncle – it can be an aunt, sibling, friend, or neighbor. These well-meaning individuals will give you advice on everything from whom you should marry, to how to raise your kids and/or how to remove a stain on your favorite shirt or blouse. The truth is, sometimes their advice isn't helpful. But don't take the know-it-all's advice without reading about the topic yourself and, more importantly, thinking for yourself. Then, when Uncle Henry gives his (usually) unsolicited advice, be polite and smile but do what you believe is the best course of action! By the way, if he tells you annuities are bad because he heard it on TV, change the channel and tune him out!

As I describe this strategy to you I suspect that you may ask the same question I have heard from countless clients. "Why has no one else told me about this?" As you may recall from an earlier chapter, I often refer to the big Wall Street firms as the "big box" Wall Street advisors. I do this because of the impersonal nature of the services they offer their clients. The big box stores work wonderfully well when it comes to delivering good products at good prices to their customers. They don't work so well in the financial advisory services that should focus on their client's individual needs and goals. At any rate, the answer is that "big box" Wall Street advisors and the banking industry have a different business model and *their model doesn't include this approach.* "Big box" Wall Street advisors have been referred to by some as the "Giant Fleecing Machine." Frankly, these firms are all about mutual fund portfolios, brokerage accounts and the tasty fees and hidden charges that come with their products. Wall Street, as Vanguard founder Jack Bogle points out, is all about *salesmanship* nowadays, it is no longer about *stewardship.* The days of Wall Street stewardship are long gone – but that won't impact those who use my Common Sense Retirement approach.

Here is what a fixed index annuity (FIA) can do for you:

1. Both before and after retirement, provide you with some of the gains of the stock market, but none of the losses.

2. Deliver to you a *guaranteed lifetime income option* that doesn't require you to give up control of your nest egg or leave your spouse or beneficiaries with nothing when you die.

3. You can select an income option that will *allow your payments to continue to grow* to offset the negative impact of inflation.

4. <u>Guarantee your retirement nest egg</u> even if, as I suspect, we enter a secular bear market. The FIA allows you to hold on to what you worked so hard to accumulate during your working life.

5. You are no longer subject to the sequence of return risk (refer back to Chapter Two) that devastated Bad Luck Bob's portfolio.

The new world of annuities

As mentioned earlier, all annuities and pensions can, if triggered, guarantee a stream of income. Why are so many consumers resistant to annuitization of all or a portion of their retirement nest egg? That is because the older annuity products were designed for a different place and time. In a time of low inflation and short life expectancies, the older annuities fit the need of most consumers. But, as Dylan sang, "the times they (were) a changin.'" It just took insurance companies a few years to catch up!

Under the older pension and annuity policies, the consumer:

1. Gave up a large lump sum of money in exchange for a lifetime of payments. If the purchaser died shortly after buying the annuity, he or she "lost" the bet.

2. Gave up all control of the amount used to purchase the lifetime of income. The amount was no longer "liquid" or immediately available in cash if a financial emergency arose.

3. At death, the payments ended. There was no opportunity to leave a legacy to loved ones or to favorite charities.

The payments were fixed; inflation eroded the value of the purchasing power of the monthly payment, month after month, year after year.

What are the chances of getting hit by a bus?

For some reason, the excuse not to annuitize used most often by consumers is: "What if the day after purchasing the annuity I get killed by a bus?" I am not sure why buses in particular fill people with such dread. Your chance of getting hit by a bus is 1 in 10 million. My source is the Internet, and we all know everything on the Internet is true!

Newer annuities have been created that supply a reliable, growing source of income without forcing annuitization. It is now possible to get annuities with *guaranteed income riders. At the same time you maintain control and may be able to leave a legacy.* Just as with automobiles, some are better than others. Some annuities are better than others. And just as new automobiles had to change with the times to meet new safety and environmental standards, annuities have changed. In other words, the insurance companies finally caught up to the changing times.

What is a rider?

In this chapter I use the term *rider.* A rider is a provision added to an annuity or insurance policy. It is not in the main policy document or contract itself. It is a benefit you can add that "rides" along with the other policy provisions. You sometimes pay extra for the rider. See my discussion below on the costs of FIAs.

Now there really *is* a better mousetrap, and here it is – the Common Sense Retirement Tool.

The FIA can offer protection from market risk, inflationary risk, and income or longevity risk in one fell swoop. Let's take a close look at my *Common Sense Retirement Tool.*

A Brief Primer on Fixed Index Annuities

I am a strong believer in the value of FIAs. In fact, I am such a strong believer they are the biggest part of my own retirement plan. As a Boomer myself (I am 67 as I write this) I searched for the best retirement tool for myself. And I found it with the FIA. Here is why.

FIAs work much like their older brothers, Fixed Annuities. The big difference (*and it is a big difference*) is that a Fixed Annuity grows when the account is credited with interest at a rate determined by the insurance company. So if the first year interest rate is 3% and the policy balance is $100,000 the account will grow by $3,000 (or 3% times $100,000). The next year the interest rate declared by the insurance company may stay the same or go up or down depending on interest rates being paid in the overall economy (nowadays interest rates generally are very low, so fixed annuities are also not paying very high interest rates).

An FIA, however, grows not by the interest rate declared at the beginning of the year by the insurance company but by the increase in a fixed index – such as the S&P 500 (refer back to Chapter Four). If the S&P

Index goes up by 10% during the year, the annuity account will grow by some portion of that. Rarely, does the account grow by the full increase (in this case, 10%) of the index, but it will grow by some portion of that – such as 55% of the increase. The amount depends on the contract you sign (a good advisor will explain these types of details to you). So, in our example, the increase will be 5.5% (or 10% times 55%). In years in which the index goes down, the increase in the account will be 0%. ***In other words, with an FIA, you get some portion of the increase of the index but none of the decrease.*** Remember when I told you I didn't hate the entire stock market – just the down part. Now you know why the FIA is my Common Sense Retirement Tool - you get to participate in some of the upside, none of the downside!

AFTERWORD

Our Cycle is Complete

How you will benefit from reading this chapter: *So now our cycle is complete. In the introduction I argued that Common Sense Retirement Planning means income is the outcome. A good retirement plan is very different from a good investment plan. An investment plan focuses on the growth of your assets and accepts risk as necessary for long-term asset growth; a good retirement plan focuses on creating a reliable, growing source of income; risk is not a welcome component. In a nutshell that is what Common Sense Retirement Planning is all about – creating a reliable, growing source of income. In a recent Harvard Business Review article, Nobel Prize-winning economist Robert Merton agreed with me that income is the right outcome.*

In the July-August 2014 issue of the Harvard Business Review, Robert Merton wrote:

"Our approach to saving is all wrong: We need to think about monthly income, not net worth." (The Crisis in Retirement Planning; Harvard Business Review, July-August 2014; available at www.hbr.org)

Indeed, that is what I've been arguing throughout my book, at some point your focus on retirement planning must change from accumulation to decumulation. No longer is growth your objective, but rather keeping what you have worked so hard to save and turning that into a stream of retirement income. I mention that age 50 is the time when that change in focus should begin for most people.

"Corporate America really started to take notice of pensions in the wake of the dot-com crash, in 2000. Interest rates and stock prices both plummeted, which meant that the value of the pension liabilities rose while the value of the assets held to meet them fell. A number of major firms in weak industries, notably steel and airlines, went bankrupt in large measure because of their inability to meet their obligations under defined-benefit pension plans. The result was an acceleration of America's shift away from defined-benefit (DB) to defined-contribution (DC) retirement plans, which transfer the retirement risk from the company to the employee. Once an add-on to traditional retirement planning, DC plans – epitomized by

the ubiquitous 401(k) – have now become the main vehicles for private retirement saving."

Revisit my history of boomer retirement in Chapter Three that recounts the same story from a slightly longer time perspective.

"The seeds of an investment crisis have been sown. The only way to avoid a catastrophe is for plan participants, professionals, and regulators to shift the mind-set and metrics from asset value to income."

I could not have summarized it better myself. See Chapter Two and Chapter Six on the role of cycles in the value of stocks and the role of the debt super cycle in creating the next investment crisis. As to Dr. Merton's comment on shifting their mind-set, that is the key to Common Sense Retirement Planning – income is the outcome!

Believe me; I am not patting myself on the back because a Nobel Prize-winning economist has concluded many of the same things I discuss in my book. And I am not implying that Dr. Merton agrees with or endorses the answer to these problems I outline in Chapter Seven. If, however, there was a Nobel Prize awarded in retirement planning, I would happily nominate Dr. Merton!

Let me leave you with one last quote from the Nobel Prize winner:

"Pension savings are invested so as to maximize capital value at the time of retirement, an objective imposed by regulation. But the goal of most savers is to achieve a reasonable level of retirement income. This mismatch almost guarantees that savings are badly managed, because an investment that is risk-free from an asset value standpoint may be very risky in income terms. At the same time, the defined contribution process requires savers who often have little or no financial expertise to make complicated decisions about risk."

OK, so Dr. Merton writes like an academic. Here it is in my simple terms:

Income is the right outcome.